Sparkle Queens
This is who we are

By Maria S. Barbo

SCHOLASTIC INC.

ISBN 978-1-339-04439-2

10 9 8 7 6 5 4 3 2 1   24 25 26 27 28

Printed in China   38
First printing 2024
Book design by Martha Maynard and Becky James

Contents

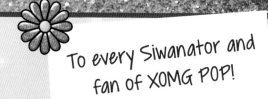

DEAR XOMG POP! FANS,

I am SO stoked for you to get to know Brooklynn, Dallas, Tinie T, and Penelope as well as I do.

These four girls are by far the most incredibly talented singers, dancers, and performers I have ever met. And I am beyond proud of every single one of them.

The work they put in is solid. Their singing and dancing is phenomenal. And their love for their fans is beyond words. Spending time with these girls and choreographing the dances for their tour has been some of the most fun I've ever had.

Each of them brings something special to the group and I cannot wait for you to see for yourselves.

XO,
JoJo

X+OMG

Triple Threat!

Where It All Began!

"X-O-M-G We making history
We superstars and together we're living the dream."

*T*ogether, Tinie T, Dallas, Brooklynn, and Penelope are living their dreams, singing from their hearts, and turning the party up in concert, in YouTube videos, and in feature films.

And their story is 100% original.

It all started when a call went out on social media to dance teachers and studios across the country looking for talented triple threats—girls who could dance, act, *and* sing. If they made the cut, they'd be on a reality show about putting together a girls' pop group. The surprise? They'd get to work with *JESS AND JOJO SIWA!*

"TRUST AND BELIEVE."
—JoJo Siwa

Thousands of kids auditioned on Zoom, twenty-one girls went to Los Angeles for in-person auditions, and eleven made it onto

> "I got the best of the best right here." —Jessalynn Siwa

the show. But only three of those brilliant, talented girls—Brooklynn, Dallas, and Tinie T—got to wear the official XOMG POP! jackets!

The group's first official public debut was in Hollywood opening for JoJo at a superfan event. And nothing can stop them now! XOMG POP! has slayed on *America's Got Talent*, toured with JoJo, and put out their own *phenomenal* album. And they are having *the best* time! Each girl sings what's in her heart and brings her own special *pop!* to the group.

For these sparkle queens, every day's another chance to light it up with girl power! And you are about to find out all about it!

Blowing Up Like Bubble Gum!

X-O-M-G MAKING HISTORY! What are the top ten MEMORABLE moments in XOMG POP! history?

1. SIWAS DANCE POP REVOLUTION
November 4, 2020 • The reality show that introduces the world to the girls who'll become XOMG POP! airs on Peacock, and the pop party begins!

2. OMG!
December 2020 • Brooklynn, Dallas, and Tinie T become official members of XOMG POP!

3. *AMERICA'S GOT TALENT*
May 31, 2022 • XOMG POP! makes it to the semifinals of *America's Got Talent* and Simon Cowell tells the girls, "I didn't like it . . . I LOVED it!"

4. TOUR WITH JOJO SIWA
January 13, 2022 –March 12, 2022 • XOMG POP! join JoJo Siwa's D.R.E.A.M. tour!

5. MALL OF AMERICA PERFORMANCE
February 18, 2023 • XOMG POP!'s first live concert ever at the Mall of America in Minnesota.

Fun Fact
The girls were originally supposed to open for JoJo but then JoJo was like, "Nuh, uh, I want you onstage with me," and made them guest performers.

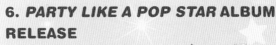

6. *PARTY LIKE A POP STAR* ALBUM RELEASE
March 10, 2023 • And it is 🔥 and 🤯!

7. PODCAST LAUNCH!
October 9, 2023 • XOMG POP! launches their first ever podcast—and it slays! ((or)) with an inside look at what it's like to be teens *and* pop stars!

8. XOMG POP! WELCOMES PENELOPE!
October 9, 2023 • Penelope LeMieux joins XOMG POP! and their vibe is complete! ((or)) and it's like the girls have known each other *1234ever*!

9. XOMG POP! CRUISE
November 10–13, 2023 • The first official XOMG POP! cruise with fans sets sail and it is *awesome*!

10. LIVE NATION TOUR
June 2024 • Fans cheer as XOMG POP! takes the stage on a cross-country tour!!

Of course, XOMG POP! have had TONS of superstar moments—like their feature film, their cartoon series, their campaign for dancers against cancer, appearances on season 11 of *Chicken Girls*, and on and on and on! The girls continue to live their dreams and make history every single day.

Fun Fact

Penelope was an extra in the "Party Like a Popstar" video before she became an official member of XOMG POP!

XOMG POP! Livin' the Dream!

A Day with the Stars

"VIPs, we're livin' that life
Every day's the day to party, party, party like . . ."

While the perfect day for the girls would for sure involve friends, family, the beach, a trip to Universal or Disney, making a *million* fun TikToks, dinner at Texas Roadhouse, or performing at the *biggest* concert for the *biggest* crowd, a regular day as an XOMG POP! star is *just* as much fun!

First of all, the girls have their *OWN HOUSE*! Yep, JoJo Siwa surprised the girls with their very own house just in time to film their "Party Like a POP STAR" video and it is . . . **Cool! Magical! Wow!**

The XOMG POP! house has a giant unicorn named Cob, a wall of fan art, a candy room, a schoolroom full of fun experiments and crafts, a bedroom for napping and chilling, a bathroom with a ball pit, and a vanity room for getting glam! And while the girls don't actually *live* in the house, it's a *super*-fun place to hang out!

The XOMG POP! stars all live with their families in Los Angeles—some even moved there just to be with the group!—and spend most days either filming YouTube content at the house *OR* rehearsing and

Sometimes our moms prep a cookout while we're filming at the XOMG POP! house so we can have a picnic during our break!

working on choreography at Siwa Studios.

Just like JoJo's mom, Jessalynn, the girls' moms are their managers and biggest supporters. And they're always on set with their girls! The moms—aka "momagers"—keep the girls on track and cheer them on from the sidelines.

So, what's it *really* like to get ready for a concert or live performance? In the weeks leading up to an event, the girls work with JoJo to learn the choreography for each song they're going to sing *and* the speaking parts that come between each song. Then there are vocal rehearsals with their coaches and costume fittings. All that can take about 7–10 days. It's a lot of work *and* a LOT of fun!

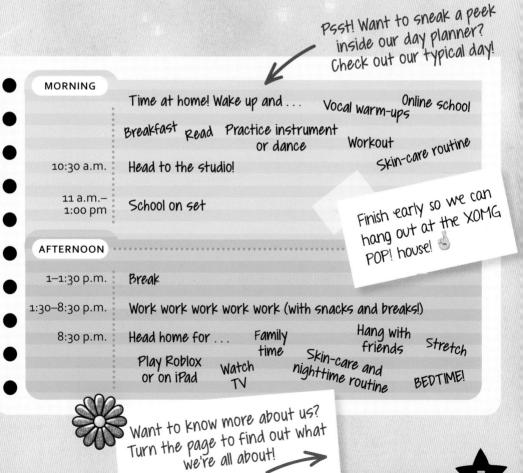

Psst! Want to sneak a peek inside our day planner? Check out our typical day!

MORNING

Time at home! Wake up and . . .   Vocal warm-ups   Online school

Breakfast   Read   Practice instrument or dance   Workout   Skin-care routine

10:30 a.m.   Head to the studio!

11 a.m.– 1:00 pm   School on set

Finish early so we can hang out at the XOMG POP! house!

AFTERNOON

1–1:30 p.m.   Break

1:30–8:30 p.m.   Work work work work work (with snacks and breaks!)

8:30 p.m.   Head home for . . .   Family time   Hang with friends   Stretch

Play Roblox or on iPad   Watch TV   Skin-care and nighttime routine   BEDTIME!

Want to know more about us? Turn the page to find out what we're all about!

That's What I'm About!
Dallas Skye

Top three words that best describe me: ➝

1️⃣ Caring

2️⃣ Smart

3️⃣ Silly

Calm

Intelligent

Funny

Bra...

Inte...

Fun Fact

Dallas's friends in XOMG Pop! describe her using all the words on this page!

8

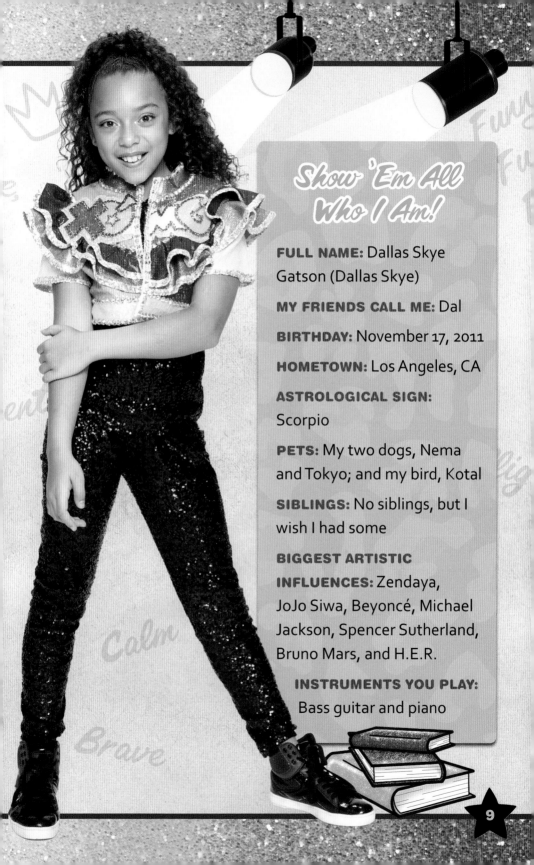

Show 'Em All Who I Am!

FULL NAME: Dallas Skye Gatson (Dallas Skye)

MY FRIENDS CALL ME: Dal

BIRTHDAY: November 17, 2011

HOMETOWN: Los Angeles, CA

ASTROLOGICAL SIGN: Scorpio

PETS: My two dogs, Nema and Tokyo; and my bird, Kotal

SIBLINGS: No siblings, but I wish I had some

BIGGEST ARTISTIC INFLUENCES: Zendaya, JoJo Siwa, Beyoncé, Michael Jackson, Spencer Sutherland, Bruno Mars, and H.E.R.

INSTRUMENTS YOU PLAY: Bass guitar and piano

Spotlight on Me!

Here's a list of my favorite things!

ICE CREAM FLAVOR: Rainbow sherbet

SNACK: Salt and vinegar chips

DINNER: Japanese bento box with onigiri, teriyaki chicken, and edamame

PIZZA TOPPING: Pepperoni

BREAKFAST: French toast, eggs, and fruit

TYPE OF CANDY: Twix

THING TO DRINK: Water and lemonade

KIND OF VACATION: Beach! I love being by the water.

COLOR: Purple, pink, and sky blue

ANIMAL: Panda

SEASON OF THE YEAR: Summer! I love the warm weather and summer nights.

SUBJECTS IN SCHOOL: Science, math, reading, and foreign languages. I love learning.

STYLE OF DANCE: Contemporary/lyrical

HOLIDAYS: Christmas! I get to spend time with my family.

MOVIES: *Hamilton* and *Jumanji* (with The Rock, Jack Black, and Kevin Hart)

TV SHOWS: *Rilakkuma and Kaoru* and *The Thundermans*

BOOK: The Dog Man and Diary of a Wimpy Kid series

WAY TO RELAX: I like to sit in my room and either listen to music or read a book.

SONG ON YOUR ALBUM: "XOMG"

LYRIC FROM ONE OF YOUR SONGS: "Bring it on let the rain come down, there ain't nothing that can stop us now" (From the song "X")

MUSIC VIDEO FROM YOUR ALBUM (AND WHY): "Party Like a POP STAR"! It literally was a big party with extras and pizza, and JoJo surprised us in the dunk tank.

SONG THAT'S NOT YOURS: "Baby Mine" from the movie *Dumbo*

BAND THAT'S NOT YOURS: The Beatles

WAY JOJO HAS SURPRISED YOU: Tokyo

Dallas is learning Japanese, Spanish, German, French, Russian, ASL (American Sign Language), and Arabic!

COSTUME TO WEAR ONSTAGE: Emmy's performance costume! The jacket reminded me of Elton John.

OUTFIT TO WEAR IN YOUR DOWNTIME: A comfy onesie

HAIR ACCESSORY: Cute hair clips

MAKEUP ITEM: Highlighter

HAIRSTYLE: Two buns or half up half down! Always rocking my natural curls.

PERFORMANCE EVER: Vidcon, because we had backup dancers!

SOLO YOU'VE EVER SUNG: "I'll Be There" by Jess Glynne

THING ABOUT BEING IN THE BAND: Traveling and performing onstage

PLACE YOU'VE PERFORMED: Caribbean / XOMG Pop! cruise

PLACE IN THE WHOLE WORLD: Tokyo and London

THING YOU OWN: My teddy bear Tayay

PRESENT YOU EVER RECEIVED: My dog, Tokyo

What's the one item I always take on the road with me? My teddy bear Tayay ♡

MANTRA, MOTTO, OR QUOTE THAT INSPIRES YOU: "What if I fall? Oh but my darling, what if you fly?" (From the poem, "What if I fall?" by Erin Hanson)

Which XOMG POP! star loves all things school, especially learning new languages?

Dazzling Diva Dallas Skye!

Dallas was only ten years old when she was cast on *Siwas Dance Pop Revolution*. She quickly became known as a big voice in a little body—a strong singer with a huge vocal range who can hit what Jessalynn Siwa calls "those big money notes."

What's guaranteed to always make me happy? When my mom makes me laugh.

Surprised? Didn't think so! Music runs in Dallas's family. "I've been around music my whole life," Dallas says, "so, I think it came naturally." Her dad sings, plays piano, and often accompanies her when she sings on social media. Her cousin Leilani also sings, and her aunts and uncles all do something related to music. "My mom and dad always knew I wanted to be a performer," Dallas notes.

What's my good luck charm? My dad gave me a heart necklace, and I keep it with me all the time. It's lucky because it reminds me he believes in me.

While Dallas is best known for her big, soulful voice, music isn't her only talent. She started dancing at age four and quickly began taking home titles from competitions. She also has four acting credits to her name, including a starring role in the XOMG POP! feature film. This sparkle queen is a true triple threat!

"Being a pop star is a lot of hard work, but I've never felt like giving up."

What makes me feel strong and confident? Believing in myself and knowing that I can do anything if I work hard enough.

Dallas *never* gives up. Her performances truly *SKYE*-rocketed once she started letting her quirky personality shine through. Like when she put her own genius spin on her solo for the JoJo Siwa

This is one of my favorite pictures. It was during my solo titled "Landslide." I was eight.

This is when I won first place for my solo at KAR (Kids Artistic Revue) nationals in Las Vegas. I was so excited!

Me and my mom on the set of Siwas Dance Pop Revolution.

Childhood Cancer Foundation fundraiser by doing ASL as she sang "What a Wonderful World." She did the song *her* way—with a ballad! And she brought. The house. Down! Jessalynn and JoJo welcomed her into the group that very night!

This superstar always *shows up*, both for her fans *and* for her friends. She's a caring friend, a good listener, a really outgoing personality, and not a surprise, she's really *funny*!

"My dog Nema (that's AMEN spelled backward!) can communicate using buttons. My dog Tokyo knows her commands in Japanese, and my bird, Kotal, can talk and play peek-a-boo!"

Dallas describes her style as *kawaii*, which means "cute" in Japanese. "I think it says I'm cute but edgy," she says. And that's

Confession Session! "Sometimes thinking about growing up makes me feel sad because I know things will be different. Talking to my mom makes me feel better."

I played Juliette in a Netflix show. I was standing outside my trailer in London.

Right before I went onstage to perform my very first solo. I was seven.

also her vibe: fun and easygoing and also grounded, curious, and wise beyond her years!

At the XOMG POP! house, Dallas spends the most time in the schoolroom, where there are lots of fun experiments and crafts. She loves science and engineering projects like building vending machines out of cardboard, teaching her pets to communicate, learning new instruments and languages, writing her own music, and following her curiosity in general.

When it comes to learning and performing, Dallas wants to slay it all! Her goals for this year are to keep

What scares me? "Having to speak on live TV was a little scary because it's one take and no do-overs."

"Don't be crazy, know you're amazing!"

Performing my solo, "Wake Me Up."

This is me and my uncle Chris.

improving her dancing and singing. And in ten years? "It would be cool to be on the list of EGOTs [Emmy, Grammy, Oscar, Tony]!"

What does the future hold for this determined dynamo? Fans and friends know that no matter what path Dallas Skye chooses, the *SKYE'S* the limit!

Who's the celebrity I admire most? Zendaya! "She's awesome because she does everything I want to do and she's super talented. I've always wanted to sing and dance with her and maybe do Carpool Karaoke."

Miss Kiana is one of my favorite dance teachers. She choreographed all my solos! She's like my big sister and I love her so much!

Me and my uncle Chris playing bass. He's the best!

 Singing for family.

Little Dallas and her dad.

Dallas with her cousin Leilani.

Dallas and her dog, Nema.

"I don't want to brag, buuuut I feel like I'm a beast."

Me and my grandpa I call Pamp. He's my best friend in the whole wide world and I love him so much.

Did Somebody Say "Slay?"

Ready for My
TOP THREE TOP THREE
Lists?

TOP THREE THINGS I LOVE MOST ABOUT MYSELF:

1. My curly hair

2. My personality

3. My laugh

TOP THREE THINGS I WANT TO LEARN OR GET BETTER AT:

1. Learning languages

2. Performing (acting, music, stage)

3. Designing my own clothes

TOP THREE TIMES I'VE FELT MOST PROUD OF MYSELF:

1. Making XOMG POP!

2. Winning nationals my first year doing a dance solo

3. Building a vending machine out of cardboard

Would You Rather . . .

- . . . Eat a burger or fries?
- . . . Do yoga or go running?
- . . . Go to dance practice or vocal practice?
- . . . Wake up to a sunny day or a rainy day?
- . . . Wear sneakers or fancy shoes?
- . . . Bike or read?
- . . . Swim or go skating?
- . . . Eat cake or cookies?
- . . . Eat ice cream or pie?
- . . . Sparkle or shine?
- . . . Wear neon or glitter?
- . . . Watch a movie that made you laugh or one that scared you a little?
- . . . Wear your hair up or down?
- . . . Wake up early or stay up late?
- . . . Tell a friend a secret or write your secrets in your journal?
- . . . Take a test or eat something gross?
- . . . Take a cruise or go to an amusement park?
- . . . Make a video for YouTube or be interviewed on TV?
- . . . Act in a movie starring you and your friends or perform in a concert with your friends?
- . . . Grant a wish or have your wish granted?
- . . . Play it safe or go full out?

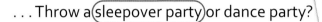

. . . Throw a sleepover party or dance party?

. . . Have a dog or a cat?

. . . Build a snowman or a sandcastle?

. . . Be the princess or the fairy godmother?

. . . Get caught in a thunderstorm or a snowstorm?

. . . Go to a movie or draw in the park?

. . . Have a vocal solo or a dance solo?

. . . Write a song or choreograph a dance?

. . . Put together a costume for a show or a skit for a video?

. . . Do a puzzle or play a board game?

. . . Roast s'mores with JoJo or throw a party at the XOMG POP! house for your fans?

. . . Take a plane to your next concert or ride in the tour bus?

. . . Be able to teleport or fly like a superhero?

. . . Be able to hear everyone's thoughts or make yourself invisible?

. . . get stuck in an elevator or up in a really tall tree?

. . . not see your BFFs for a month or not shower for a month?

. . . Act in a live-action movie or do the voice of a character in a cartoon series?

. . . Have a pillow fight or play video games?

XOMG POP! Quiz! What Animals Are We Most Like Inside?

"A Unicorn. I'm magical on the inside."

"A baby tiger because I am fierce, playful, and full of energy."

"A giraffe because they are super peaceful and clever."

"A tiger because tigers are very smart, quick, and protective. They are also very kindhearted, passionate, and loyal."

Brooklynn

That's What I'm About!
Brooklynn Pitts

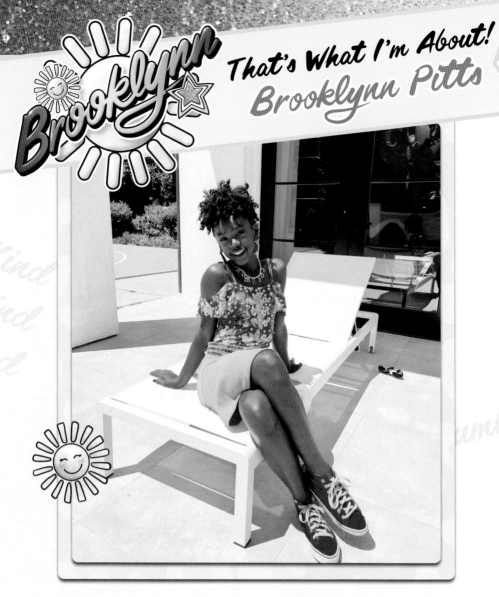

Top three words that best describe me:

1 Confident
2 Humble
3 Honest

Fun Fact
Brooklynn's friends in XOMG Pop! describe her using all the words on this page!

Show 'Em All Who I Am!

FULL NAME: Brooklynn Anne-Marie Pitts

MY FRIENDS CALL ME: Brook

BIRTHDAY: September 28, 2010

HOMETOWN: Fort Worth, TX

ASTROLOGICAL SIGN: Libra

PETS: My dogs, Sky and Hope

SIBLINGS: Jeremiah and Aniyah

BIGGEST ARTISTIC INFLUENCES: Beyoncé, BTS, ITZY, Michael Jackson, TWICE, P1Harmony, NCT DREAM

INSTRUMENTS YOU PLAY: Electric guitar, piano, and voice

Spotlight on Me!

Here's a list of my favorite things!

ICE CREAM FLAVOR: Butter pecan

SNACK: Rice cakes

DINNER: Seafood

PIZZA TOPPING: Pepperoni

BREAKFAST: Peanut butter toast

TYPE OF CANDY: Trollis, Mike and Ikes

THING TO DRINK: Sprite, water, and Coca-Cola

KIND OF VACATION: Florida, Universal, Disney World/ Disneyland, Laguna Beach, and Santa Monica Beach/Pier

COLOR: Yellow

ANIMAL: Giraffe

SEASON OF THE YEAR: Spring and summer

SUBJECTS IN SCHOOL: Math and Science

STYLE OF DANCE: Jazz

HOLIDAYS: My birthday or Christmas

MOVIES: *Aladdin*

TV SHOWS: *Dance Mom*s

BOOK: *K-Pop Revolution* by Stephan Lee and *Flying Solo* by Ralph J. Fletcher

WAY TO RELAX: Lying down in my bed

SONG ON YOUR ALBUM: "Moves"

LYRIC FROM ONE OF YOUR SONGS: "Sunshine by day, living that way, turn into a star by night."

MUSIC VIDEO FROM YOUR ALBUM (AND WHY): "Disco Believer," because I loved how the style was the '70s, and it was really cool understanding and learning about how they danced!

SONG THAT'S NOT YOURS: "Remember the Time" by Michael Jackson

BAND THAT'S NOT YOURS: NewJeans

WAY JOJO HAS SURPRISED YOU: The XOMG POP! house!

COSTUME TO WEAR ONSTAGE: Mall of America costume!

Puppy Power! "My dogs, Sky and Hope, are my super dogs. When I need comfort, I have Sky, and when I'm in a playful mood, I always need Hope."

OUTFIT TO WEAR IN YOUR DOWNTIME: Parachute pants and oversized shirts with long sleeves under it

HAIR ACCESSORY: Clips, headbands

MAKEUP ITEM: Dior lip oil and mascara

HAIRSTYLE: Bantu knots, frohawk, half Afro (slick side)

THING ABOUT BEING IN THE BAND: Traveling, going out to eat, and performing

PLACE YOU'VE PERFORMED: JoJo Siwa D.R.E.A.M. The Tour

PLACE IN THE WHOLE WORLD: Korea, Tokyo, Paris

THING YOU OWN: My electric guitar

PRESENT YOU EVER RECEIVED: My K-pop albums

MANTRA, MOTTO, OR QUOTE THAT INSPIRES YOU: "Love yourself, because there is no one like you," from the poem, "I'm a Fan of Me," by Tre King

PERFORMANCE EVER: Mall of America, because it was the first time we got to do more than one song!

SOLO YOU'VE EVER SUNG: "The Climb" by Miley Cyrus

Brooklynn

Brooklynn Pitts!

W hen Jessalynn Siwa first saw Brooklynn, she had a feeling this sparkle queen from Texas was going to be one of *Siwas Dance Pop Revolution*'s strongest all-around girls—a singer, dancer, nice kid, performer, and animated to boot. Everyone loves Brooklynn! Not a surprise. Brooklynn's always bringing the superstar vibes!

Like all the girls in XOMG POP!, Brooklynn began her career young—singing in church, doing voice lessons, going on auditions, and dancing competitively. "Ever since I was two, my parents said I was gonna be a star," Brooklynn says, "and when I started singing and entering dance competitions, we realized that performing was the thing for me."

My lucky charm is my voice because I feel like I have a great gift, and I would love to show the world my gift.

What's my happy place? My room. When I'm in my room, I feel relaxed and calm.

31

The truth is, Brooklynn works hard and lights up the stage. Her mom, a former dancer, had always wanted Brooklynn to try dance, but the first time was a no-go. Little Brooklynn hated it! Fast-forward a couple of years, and they tried again. As her mom said on the show, "That's when the fire came out!" and it was clear performing would be Brooklynn's passion.

"My mother inspires me the most because of how hardworking and loving she is. She pushes me but that's what I love about her."

This is my cousin Lindsay, who dances with the Dance Theatre of Harlem in New York. She has always supported my dance journey.

"My fans make me more confident; they are so sweet. I also think my mother encourages me to be confident no matter what."

Brooklynn admits she struggles sometimes. There are moments when her nerves get the best of her! But Brooklynn doesn't let it get her down. "Sometimes when we have a bad rehearsal, I feel like I wanna give up," she says. "But I always tell myself to keep going no matter what happens." Her fans are glad she does! Because when Brooklynn finds her confidence, she performs at a level Jessalynn Siwa calls "unreal."

My first dance teacher, Mrs. Nina. She never let me quit and always gave me encouraging words.

What is guaranteed to always make me feel happy? My friends and family.

My regional dance competition, where I received first overall.

This was my second solo to Michael Jackson. It was so challenging, but Mrs. Nina always believed in me and pushed me harder.

What makes Brooklynn a standout? "Being comfortable in the skin I'm in," Brooklynn says. "My signature look would have to be my natural hair (any style), sunshine, stars, and affirmations. I feel like it really shows that I want to inspire people to be themselves, or who they wanna be." And who does Brooklynn want to be? Herself, of course! And it's that down-to-earth, peaceful attitude that allows her to be an honest, funny, and loyal friend to her girls in XOMG POP!

Want to know a secret I haven't told my friends . . . yet?! I play electric guitar and I like making beats and music.

This was one of my favorite solos choreographed by Mrs. Nina. I was so excited.

What gets me pumped up when I'm down? "Listening to upbeat music like Kendrick Lamar or K-pop. It always works."

This is Mrs. Nina at my very first national dance competition, where I took first overall in my category.

Brooklynn was the second girl to get her jacket on *Siwas Dance Pop Revolution*, and she's never looked back. At the XOMG POP! house, she can be found doing "Cook with Brook" videos for their YouTube channel, laughing with her friends, and giving her body the rest it needs. As Brooklynn's confessed, "I spend the most time in the bedroom because I loooovvvvvve sleeping."

As her star continues to rise, Brooklynn strives to grow more and more confident in her skills onstage. Ten years from now, she sees herself still performing and making music, and that's what her fans are livin' for!

This was my second year of my dance season receiving first place in my category and first place overall at my very first dance convention.

This was my last year competing in a dance competition before moving to California.

This is my little sister, Aniyah, who would hang out with me backstage.

Me and my mom; dad; brother, Jeremiah; and sister, Aniyah.

"I miss my grandparents a lot because I used to see them every day, or they would come to all of my performances. Now that we moved to California, they can't."

LOVING

Look for Sunshine till I Find It!

Here's My TOP THREE TOP THREE List!

TOP THREE THINGS I LOVE MOST ABOUT MYSELF:

1. My gratitude
2. My confidence
3. My determination

TOP THREE THINGS I WANT TO LEARN OR GET BETTER AT:

1. Singing
2. Electric guitar
3. Acting

TOP THREE TIMES I'VE FELT MOST PROUD OF MYSELF:

1. When I made it into XOMG POP!
2. When I finished Mall of America
3. When I overcame my nervousness

Would You Rather . . .

- . . . Eat a burger or fries?
- . . . Do yoga or go running?
- . . . Go to dance practice or vocal practice?
- . . . Wake up to a sunny day or a rainy day?
- . . . Wear sneakers or fancy shoes?
- . . . Bike or read?
- . . . Swim or go skating?
- . . . Eat cake or cookies?
- . . . Eat ice cream or pie?
- . . . Sparkle or shine?
- . . . Wear neon or glitter?
- . . . Watch a movie that made you laugh or one that scared you a little?
- . . . Wear your hair up or down?
- . . . Wake up early or stay up late?
- . . . Tell a friend a secret or write your secrets in your journal?
- . . . Take a test or eat something gross?
- . . . Take a cruise or go to an amusement park?
- . . . Make a video for YouTube or be interviewed on TV?
- . . . Act in a movie starring you and your friends or perform in a concert with your friends?
- . . . Grant a wish or have your wish granted?
- . . . Play it safe or go full out?

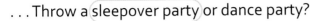

. . . Throw a sleepover party or dance party?

. . . Have a dog or a cat?

. . . Build a snowman or a sandcastle?

. . . Be the princess or the fairy godmother?

. . . Get caught in a thunderstorm or a snowstorm?

. . . Go to a movie or draw in the park?

. . . Have a vocal solo or a dance solo?

. . . Write a song or choreograph a dance?

. . . Put together a costume for a show or a skit for a video?

. . . Do a puzzle or play a board game?

. . . Roast s'mores with JoJo or throw a party at the XOMG POP! house for your fans?

. . . Take a plane to your next concert or ride in the tour bus?

. . . Be able to teleport or fly like a superhero?

. . . Be able to hear everyone's thoughts or make yourself invisible?

. . . get stuck in an elevator or up in a really tall tree?

. . . not see your BFFs for a month or not shower for a month?

. . . Act in a live-action movie or do the voice of a character in a cartoon series?

. . . Have a pillow fight or play video games?

Be Yourself and Don't Pretend!

What makes us laugh harder than anything else?

"When I watch myself fall on a video."

"I love watching my dog getting a new toy, and watching my dog wrap himself into a blanket burrito."

"When my dog does his 'zoomies' and runs around the house."

"Farts make me laugh!! So do jokes and just being silly. Also, being with the girls. They are so funny and when we're together, all we do is laugh."

What makes us cry *every* time?

"I'll cry if I lose Tayay."

"I can't really think of anything that would make me cry."

"When I found out BTS went into the army."

"I am not a big crier, but usually when I scrape my knee or hurt myself."

Tinie T

That's What I'm About!
Tinie T

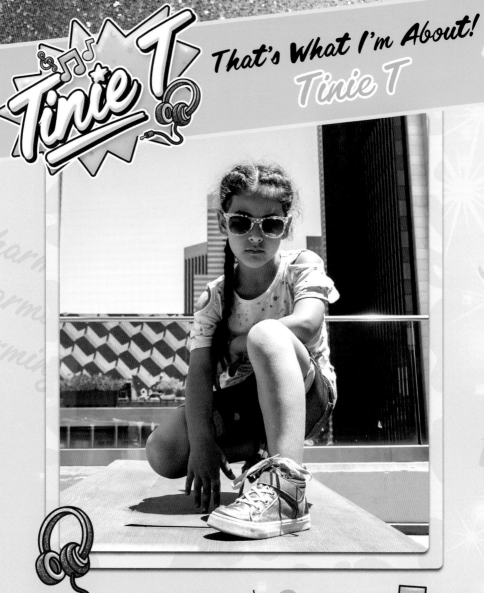

Top three words that best describe me:

1. Chill
2. Charming
3. Swaggy

Fun Fact

Tinie T's friends in XOMG Pop! describe her using all the words on this page!

Show 'Em All Who She Is!

FULL NAME: Tamara Andreasyan (Tinie T)

MY FRIENDS CALL ME: Tinie T

BIRTHDAY: March 13, 2011

HOMETOWN: Los Angeles, California

ASTROLOGICAL SIGN: Pisces

PETS: A pit bull named Tyson!

SIBLINGS: My older brother, Hamlet

ARTISTIC INFLUENCES: SZA, Rihanna, Frank Ocean, Eminem, Tupac, Drake, Kendrick Lamar, Tyler The Creator, and Bruno Mars

INSTRUMENTS YOU PLAY: Electric guitar, piano, drums

Spotlight on Me!

Here's a list of my favorite things!

ICE CREAM FLAVOR: Vanilla, because it is plain and simple

SNACK: Lime-flavored Lays chips

DINNER: Sushi

PIZZA TOPPING: Pepperoni

BREAKFAST: Cereal, oatmeal, and bagels with cream cheese

TYPE OF CANDY: Hershey's milk chocolate bars

THING TO DRINK: Water

KIND OF VACATION: Beach

COLOR: Blue, black, white, lavender, and wine red

ANIMAL: Black panthers and dolphins

SEASON OF THE YEAR: Summer

SUBJECTS IN SCHOOL: Science

STYLE OF DANCE: Hip-hop

HOLIDAY: Christmas

Fun Fact Tinie loves boogie boarding and skateboarding!

MOVIE: *Murder Mystery*

TV SHOW: *Outer Banks*

BOOK: *Johnny Tremain* by Esther Forbes and *The Outsiders* by S. E. Hinton

WAY TO RELAX: I like to play my electric guitar 🎸 as a way to relax

SONG ON YOUR ALBUM: "Disco Believer" and "Rock the Night"

LYRIC FROM ONE OF YOUR SONGS: "Yo, what up, its Tinie T from Merry Go Round"

MUSIC VIDEO FROM YOUR ALBUM (AND WHY): "Disco Believer," because it was based off the '70s and we got to dress like we were in the '70s

BAND THAT'S NOT YOURS: TLC and Destiny's Child

SONGS: "Seek & Destroy" by SZA, "Pink + White" by Frank Ocean, "Dear Mama" by Tupac Shakur, and "Please Don't Stop the Music" by Rihanna

WAY JOJO HAS SURPRISED YOU: When she told us we were coming on tour with her

COSTUME TO WEAR ONSTAGE: Our cruise costume

OUTFIT TO WEAR IN YOUR DOWNTIME: Sweatpants and a T-shirt or hoodie

HAIR ACCESSORY: Hair tie

MAKEUP ITEM: Mascara

HAIRSTYLE: Hair down, a ponytail, or braids

STANDOUT ACCESSORY: Chains, necklaces, bracelets, earrings, and rings

PERFORMANCE EVER: "The Ellen Show"

SOLO YOU'VE EVER SUNG: "Dear Mama" by Tupac Shakur

THING ABOUT BEING IN THE BAND: Traveling

PLACE YOU'VE PERFORMED: Mall of America

PLACE IN THE WHOLE WORLD: Egypt, Dubai, and Venice

THING YOU OWN: Beats by Dre headphones

PRESENT YOU EVER RECEIVED: Electric guitar

MANTRA, MOTTO, OR QUOTE THAT INSPIRES YOU: "Hard work beats talent when talent doesn't work hard." - Tim Notke

Which XOMG POP! star is a prankster who loves to make everyone laugh?

"It's Your Girl Tinie T Here!"

Even as a tiny tot, Tinie T's talent was clear. "I think the age where I was able to walk, I started dancing and singing in our living room," she says. "And that was the moment my parents knew I was going to be a pop star. So, they started taking me to different dance classes, which is when I realized that I enjoyed it very much and wanted to pursue it professionally."

This dancing queen danced competitively for a full year before appearing on *Siwas Dance Pop Revolution*, but her flexibility—and amazing back handsprings—come from her early days as a rhythmic gymnast! Tinie T competed in floor routines set to music, using props like a hoop, ribbon, ball, clubs, and rope.

Tinie T may have stolen the show in gymnastics and dance competitions, but it's rapping that has always come the most naturally to her. "Rihanna, Eminem, and 2Pac inspire me most," she says. "People didn't really expect a six-year-old

What is guaranteed to always make me feel happy? When I come home and see my family, I'm happy.

Do you like my moves? Guess what? I'm double-jointed!

49

Recording a cover to a song.

to rap, or even know rappers like 2Pac and Eminem, but they have always been a big inspiration to me. And Rihanna is an extremely successful female artist in this crazy industry, and I like her a lot—not only as a singer but also as a funny and kind human being."

If I could spend the day with someone famous . . . I would spend the day with Rihanna, because I've always loved her music and she is one of my role models.

The biggest moment in Tinie T's career came when she performed with *the* Taylor Swift at the American Music Awards in 2019. Tinie T's sportiness and rapping skills made her a standout from day one. But it was her passion, perseverance, and kindheartedness that got her a spot in XOMG POP!

Filming a scene from one of my covers called "Man's Not Hot."

That doesn't mean the road to stardom was all glitter and mic drops. "At one point in my life, I considered giving up on becoming a pop star because it's not easy working in this industry," she says. "There are hundreds of kids who also want to pursue what I wanted to be. One day I realized that being a pop star is what I've always wanted, and so I will always keep on pushing to become the best version of myself."

Tinie T definitely had a few off days on *Siwas Dance Pop Revolution*, and even got passed over for a rap solo! But she didn't let her disappointment affect her performance. Tinie T went onstage and showed the world who she is by dancing and singing backup full out!

When the frustrations and disappointments come—and they always do!—Tinie T remembers that every performance is a learning experience. "I focus on the positive,"

What makes Tinie T feel strong and confident? Knowing that no matter what, my family is always going to be there for me.

Getting ready to do a fun runway show during my friend's birthday party.

What do I miss most when I'm on tour? My pit bull, Tyson! "He is a guard dog, which makes him very protective and loyal, but he is also SUPER ENERGETIC and he LOVES his toys.

she says. "Even if I didn't get the lead role, I'm still an important part of the performance! Every member of the group contributes to making the show a success."

And when Tinie T pulled on her sequined XOMG POP! jacket for the first time, she was touched that it was her personality that had sealed the deal. "Now that I'm finally here I'm like, they wanted me for me," she said after making the group. "They want me to be who I am. It just feels amazing."

Posing on the red carpet at the American Music Awards! ➡️

Rehearsing my routine during one of my gymnastics competitions.

Performing at our local church event.

Now Royal T is living her dreams, making history, and delivering the best version of herself to fans! She gets to rap, sing, and dance onstage with four of her best friends—AND be in videos, films, and animation. She's also acted in the Lebanese version of the TV show *Little Big Shots*.

At the XOMG POP! house, Tinie T brings the laughs *and* the love. She can be found freestyling—making up raps without planning or memorization—hosting hip-hop-inspired fashion shows, choreographing moves and dance challenges for social media posts, and planning clever new pranks to play on her friends. (Did somebody say confetti cannon?) And the best part is she gets to do it all with her four best friends.

I auditioned to be on America's Got Talent.

My family holiday card!
That's me, my parents,
and my brother, Hamlet.

I've always loved
performing!

I ride horses!

My first communion.

Having fun at a carnival game at the Santa Monica Pier.

Halloween trick or treat at the mall.

Practicing for my video of the "Old Town Road" cover.

Come On, Step On Up, This Is Your Turn.

Ready to Read My
TOP THREE TOP THREE Lists?

TOP THREE TIMES I FELT MOST PROUD OF MYSELF:

1. On tour with JoJo

2. When we appeared on *The Ellen Show*

3. When we performed with Taylor Swift at the American Music Awards in 2019

TOP THREE THINGS I WANT TO LEARN OR GET BETTER AT:

1. My vocals

2. My acting

3. Electric guitar

TOP THREE THINGS I LOVE MOST ABOUT MYSELF:

1. I'm always respectful toward others.

2. I'm humble.

3. I'm honest.

Would You Rather . . .

- . . . Eat a burger or fries?
- . . . Do yoga or go running?
- . . . Go to dance practice or vocal practice?
- . . . Wake up to a sunny day or a rainy day?
- . . . Wear sneakers or fancy shoes?
- . . . Bike or read?
- . . . Swim or go skating?
- . . . Eat cake or cookies?
- . . . Eat ice cream or pie?
- . . . Sparkle or shine?
- . . . Wear neon or glitter?
- . . . Watch a movie that made you laugh or one that scared you a little?
- . . . Wear your hair up or down?
- . . . Wake up early or stay up late?
- . . . Tell a friend a secret or write your secrets in your journal?
- . . . Take a test or eat something gross?
- . . . Take a cruise or go to an amusement park?
- . . . Make a video for YouTube or be interviewed on TV?
- . . . Act in a movie starring you and your friends or perform in a concert with your friends?
- . . . Grant a wish or have your wish granted?
- . . . Play it safe or go full out?

- . . . Throw a sleepover party or dance party?
- . . . Have a dog or a cat?
- . . . Build a snowman or a sandcastle?
- . . . Be the princess or the fairy godmother?
- . . . Get caught in a thunderstorm or a snowstorm?
- . . . Go to a movie or draw in the park?
- . . . Have a vocal solo or a dance solo?
- . . . Write a song or choreograph a dance?
- . . . Put together a costume for a show or a skit for a video?
- . . . Do a puzzle or play a board game?
- . . . Roast s'mores with JoJo or throw a party at the XOMG POP! house for your fans?
- . . . Take a plane to your next concert or ride in the tour bus?
- . . . Be able to teleport or fly like a superhero?
- . . . Be able to hear everyone's thoughts or make yourself invisible?
- . . . get stuck in an elevator or up in a really tall tree?
- . . . not see your BFFs for a month or not shower for a month?
- . . . Act in a live-action movie or do the voice of a character in a cartoon series?
- . . . Have a pillow fight or play video games?

Confession Session

Extra, Extra, We're All About It

Penelope

WHAT IS . . .

. . . **YOUR WORST HABIT?** Biting my nails

. . . **YOUR BEST HABIT?** I am very dedicated to practicing.

. . . **THE GROSSEST THING YOU'VE EVER EATEN?**
Mustard and a grape, because my friend dared me to

. . . **YOUR BIGGEST FEAR?** Bees. Period!

. . . **YOUR BIGGEST DREAM? TO** meet Taylor Swift and win
a Grammy!

Dallas

WHAT IS . . .

. . . **YOUR WORST HABIT?** Being on my phone

. . . **YOUR BEST HABIT?** Drinking water

. . . **THE GROSSEST THING YOU'VE EVER EATEN?**
A dog-food-flavored jellybean

. . . **YOUR BIGGEST FEAR?** Being on an elevator and it falling

. . . **YOUR BIGGEST DREAM?** Being in a movie with Zendaya

Tinie T

WHAT IS . . .

. . . YOUR WORST HABIT? Biting my nails

. . . YOUR BEST HABIT? If I do something, I will do it over and over again until it's perfect.

. . . THE GROSSEST THING YOU'VE EVER EATEN? I tried baby food again when I was twelve.

. . . YOUR BIGGEST FEAR? Loneliness

. . . YOUR BIGGEST DREAM? become a household name worldwide as a performing artist

Brooklynn

WHAT IS . . .

. . . YOUR WORST HABIT? Biting my nails and my cuticles

. . . YOUR BEST HABIT? I drink lots of water

. . . THE GROSSEST THING YOU'VE EVER EATEN? An anchovy

. . . YOUR BIGGEST FEAR? Elevators

. . . YOUR BIGGEST DREAM? To go to the Grammys

61

Penelope

That's What I'm About!
Penelope

Top three words that best describe me:

1. Sweet
2. Funny
3. Loud

Fun Fact Penelope's friends in XOMG Pop! describe her using all the words on this page!

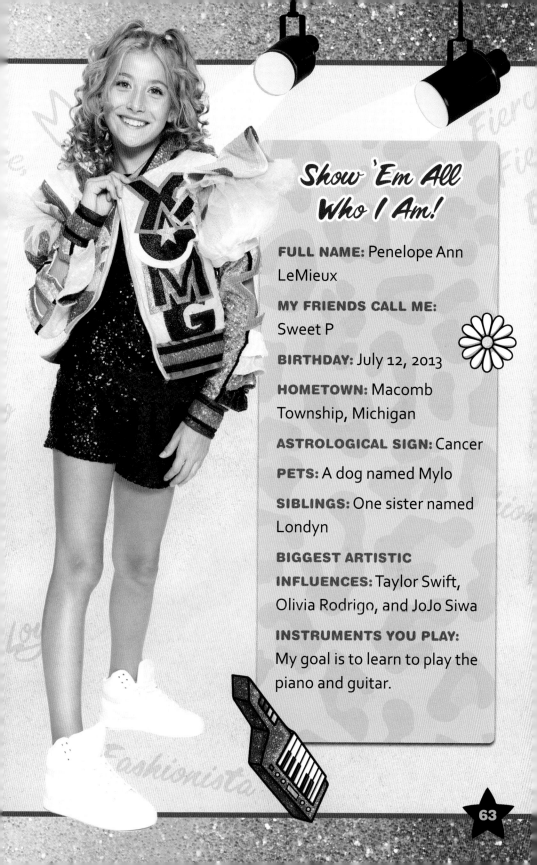

Show 'Em All Who I Am!

FULL NAME: Penelope Ann LeMieux

MY FRIENDS CALL ME: Sweet P

BIRTHDAY: July 12, 2013

HOMETOWN: Macomb Township, Michigan

ASTROLOGICAL SIGN: Cancer

PETS: A dog named Mylo

SIBLINGS: One sister named Londyn

BIGGEST ARTISTIC INFLUENCES: Taylor Swift, Olivia Rodrigo, and JoJo Siwa

INSTRUMENTS YOU PLAY: My goal is to learn to play the piano and guitar.

63

Spotlight on Me!

Here's a list of my favorite things!

ICE-CREAM FLAVOR: Vanilla and cookie dough

SNACK: Baked green pea snacks

DINNER: Any type of pasta!

PIZZA TOPPING: Cheese and pineapple

BREAKFAST: Eggs and toast

TYPE OF CANDY: Any type of sour gummies (Trolli Sour Brite Octopus gummies, to be exact)

THING TO DRINK: Pink lemonade and Dr. Pepper

KIND OF VACATION: Anywhere tropical and warm

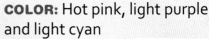

COLOR: Hot pink, light purple and light cyan

ANIMAL: Dog

SEASON OF THE YEAR: Summer

SUBJECTS IN SCHOOL: Art and science. I love crafts and experiments!

STYLE OF DANCE: Hip-hop, jazz funk, and jazz

HOLIDAY: Christmas

MOVIE: *Titanic*

TV SHOW: *Friends*

BOOK: The Harry Potter series

WAY TO RELAX: Staying in my pajamas, in my tent with snacks, playing Roblox!

SONG ON YOUR ALBUM: "Disco Believer"

LYRIC FROM ONE OF YOUR SONGS: "Don't listen to all the hate that you hear, my friend." (From the song "You Can Be Anything")

MUSIC VIDEO FROM YOUR ALBUM (AND WHY): "Party Like a Popstar" because that was my first XOMG POP! Music Video and it holds special meaning

SONG THAT'S NOT YOURS: Taylor Swift's "Cruel Summer"

BAND THAT'S NOT YOURS: BTS

WAY JOJO HAS SURPRISED YOU: When she surprises us with new bakery items every day. They are so yummy!

COSTUME TO WEAR ONSTAGE: Original XOMG Pop! Jacket and pink sequin skirt

OUTFIT TO WEAR IN YOUR DOWNTIME: Sweatpants, T-shirt, and Ugg slippers

I have a white Bichon named Mylo. He is special because he is the most cuddly and loveable dog ever. He also LOVES to play a lot like I do.

HAIR ACCESSORY: Any cute bow and a claw clip

MAKEUP ITEM: Mascara and highlighter

HAIRSTYLE: Hair down/natural curls

I LOVE doing my own hair and makeup every day! It makes me so happy and I feel very creative.

PERFORMANCE EVER: The XOMG POP! Cruise, for sure!

SOLO YOU'VE EVER SUNG: "Vampire" by Olivia Rodrigo

THING ABOUT BEING IN THE BAND: How much fun I have with the girls and JoJo

PLACE YOU'VE PERFORMED: The XOMG Pop! Cruise

PLACE IN THE WHOLE WORLD: I have never been, but I would LOVE to go to Australia

THING YOU OWN: My phone

PRESENT YOU EVER RECEIVED: My Dog 100%

"My favorite costume is probably the original XOMG POP! jacket because that was the first one I received when I joined the group and it felt official and made me so happy!"

MANTRA, MOTTO, OR QUOTE THAT INSPIRES YOU: "Be the best version of yourself."

"My favorite thing to do with my family is play card games and go to our family cabin."

Which XOMG POP! star has JoJo called "sweet," "awesome," and a "little firecracker"? the youngest—and newest—member of XOMG POP!

Penelope LeMieux

L ike the other girls in XOMG POP!, Penelope got her start in the competitive dance world. "I would dance everywhere," Penelope says, "even in the grocery store. I always knew this was something I wanted to do."

"If I could be known for one thing, it would be that I'm kind to everyone."

Penelope got America's attention when she took the stage of *America's Got Talent* with Phil Wright and Parent Jam, a group of parents and kids who dance together. And she *totally* stole the show!

But do you know how she got her start with XOMG POP!? As an extra in the "Party Like a Popstar" video! And when JoJo and Jessalynn saw her audition reel—after watching literally THOUSANDS of submissions!—they knew right away they'd found the newest member of XOMG POP!

Fun fact! Penelope met JoJo for the first time at the "Party Like a Popstar" music video filming at the XOMG POP! house—right as JoJo was getting dunked in the dunk tank! "As soon as I saw her I was like, 'Am I dreaming? What is really happening right now?'"

67

My very first dance recital and I was two years old.

After all, it takes a super-talented, super-driven girl to share the stage with Dallas, Tinie T, and Brooklynn! "Penelope seemed like the perfect fit," JoJo said. "She's a little firecracker. She's awesome."

Was it hard to be the XOMG POP! new girl? Um, sorta . . . "I was so nervous!" Penelope told fans on her first ever episode of the *XOMG POP! PODCAST*. "But it wasn't my first time being the new girl." In fourth grade, Penelope went to public school for the first time after being homeschooled. "I walked into the classroom and this girl was sitting right in front of me and she was like, 'Hi, wanna be friends?'"

What does it mean to be brave? "To know who YOU are and to not be shy to share that with the world!"

My very first solo, "Great Balls of Fire" when I was five years old. This was at JUMP Dance Convention.

My very first 24 Seven Dance Convention. I was five years old and it got me hooked on dance conventions.

What about when things get hard? "I've never really wanted to give up. But I've needed my mom and my girls to remind me that I am enough!"

So when Penelope and her mom showed up to her very first XOMG POP! rehearsal and saw Dallas walk by their car, Penelope knew what to do. "I walked up to Dallas and was like, 'Hi, do you want to be friends?'"

Penelope, Dallas, Tinie T, and Brooklynn clicked from the very first day. "It also helped because I feel like we have the same personality and humor and stuff," Penelope says. "So, I just adapted really quickly."

Penelope keeps a positive attitude—even when times are tough. Or when her jacket zipper gets stuck and she misses her cue? (Yikes!) "There are times when I feel a little nervous before a performance, but I've never been sad or afraid." When things

What's the BEST part of being in XOMG POP! for Penelope? "EVERYTHING! It is such a positive and FUN experience!" she says. "I love what I do!"

don't go as she'd hoped, Penelope tries to remember that everyone has their own time to shine! "My good luck charm is prayer," Penelope says. "I turn to God for everything!"

Aside from hard work and prayer, Penelope knows her mom is the reason for her success. "My mom has sacrificed so much for me and is my biggest supporter," Penelope says. "What she does for me and my sister is unreal."

Family and friends come first for this firecracker. "My happy place is home with family, either in California or Michigan," she notes. "My mom and my grandma make me feel strong and confident because they're supportive and always there for me. And my grandpa (aka Bub Bubs) and I have a very special bond. I love him so much! And I know they will always love me, no matter what."

Penelope's vibe is all pink heart emoji, fire emoji, silly face emoji and her style is fun, girly, and pink. She loves wearing bright, bouncy skirts onstage, but she's more of a sweatpants-and-Uggs kind of girl in her downtime.

If you want to find this artsy star in the XOMG POP! house, she'll be crafting, doing

This was at a 24 Seven Dance Convention and I won the full scholarship called Non-Stop Dancer Winner.

My eight-year-old solo "Business of Love." This was one of my favorite solos ever. This was at NUVO Dance Convention and I received first overall.

What does Penelope struggle with most in practice or onstage? "I would say endurance. It's something that I continue to work on daily."

experiments, or testing out new looks in front of the makeup mirror! "I LOVE doing my own hair and makeup every day!" Penelope notes. "It makes me so happy and I feel very creative."

What talent will Penelope LeMieux tackle next? For now, Penelope's goals are to continue to grow in dancing and singing and to get better at piano and maybe learn another instrument. And ten years from now? "I see myself also playing the guitar and being a household name."

Of course, her fans know—she already is!

My mom and I were on America's Got Talent with a group called Phil Wright and the Parent Jam. We had the best time ever. Being able to dance with my mom is a moment I will never forget.

I was JoJo Siwa for Halloween. I was and still am her biggest fan.

My sister and I being silly at our cabin in Northern Michigan.

Fans might be surprised to learn I am fifty percent Mexican. This is me making tamales on Christmas Eve with my family.

This is my mom, Kristine, and my older sister, Londyn.

This is my mom, dad (Papi), sister (Londyn), and me being silly.

I was a flower girl at my Aunt Whitney's wedding.

Buckle Up!

Here Are My
TOP THREE TOP THREE
Lists!

TOP THREE THINGS I LOVE ABOUT MYSELF:

1. My curly hair
2. My humor
3. My soft spot for older people

TOP THREE THINGS I WANT TO LEARN OR GET BETTER AT:

1. Piano
2. Hair
3. Math

TOP THREE TIMES I'VE FELT MOST PROUD OF MYSELF:

1. Teaching my dog all of his tricks
2. The first time I did my own rhinestones
3. When I became the new member of XOMG POP!

Would You Rather . . .

. . . Eat a burger or fries?

. . . Do yoga or go running?

. . . Go to dance practice or vocal practice?

. . . Wake up to a sunny day or a rainy day?

. . . Wear sneakers or fancy shoes?

. . . Bike or read?

. . . Swim or go skating?

. . . Eat cake or cookies?

. . . Eat ice cream or pie?

. . . Sparkle or shine?

. . . Wear neon or glitter?

. . . Watch a movie that made you laugh or one that scared you a little?

. . . Wear your hair up or down?

. . . Wake up early or stay up late?

. . . Tell a friend a secret or write your secrets in your journal?

. . . Take a test or eat something gross?

. . . Take a cruise or go to an amusement park?

. . . Make a video for YouTube or be interviewed on TV?

. . . Act in a movie starring you and your friends or perform in a concert with your friends?

. . . Grant a wish or have your wish granted?

. . . Play it safe or go full out?

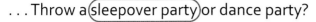

. . . Throw a sleepover party or dance party?

. . . Have a dog or a cat?

. . . Build a snowman or a sandcastle?

. . . Be the princess or the fairy godmother?

. . . Get caught in a thunderstorm or a snowstorm?

. . . Go to a movie or draw in the park?

. . . Have a vocal solo or a dance solo?

. . . Write a song or choreograph a dance?

. . . Put together a costume for a show or a skit for a video?

. . . Do a puzzle or play a board game?

. . . Roast s'mores with JoJo or throw a party at the XOMG POP! house for your fans?

. . . Take a plane to your next concert or ride in the tour bus?

. . . Be able to teleport or fly like a superhero?

. . . Be able to hear everyone's thoughts or make yourself invisible?

. . . get stuck in an elevator or up in a really tall tree?

. . . not see your BFFs for a month or not shower for a month?

. . . Act in a live-action movie or do the voice of a character in a cartoon series?

. . . Have a pillow fight or play video games?

Dream Birthdays

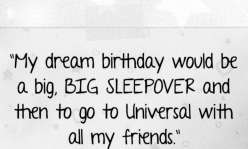

Wanna hear about our best birthdays and dream birthdays?

"My dream birthday would be a big, BIG SLEEPOVER and then to go to Universal with all my friends."

Brooklynn

"My dream birthday party would be on a tropical island with unlimited slushies and all of my friends and family."

Penelope

"My dream birthday would be to go to Tokyo with my friends and family and visit the Capybara Café and Tokyo Disneyland!"

"My dream birthday would be on a private beach with all of my family and friends. We would go swimming, boogie boarding, and after that we would roast s'mores, play board games, and watch the sunset."

Magical Powers

If we could have one magical power,
what would we choose?

"To make everyone in the world happy."

Brooklynn

"To teleport so I could travel all over the world. I love traveling and meeting cool new people."

Dallas

"To end poverty and hunger in the whole entire word."

Tinie T

"To teleport, because I am not a fan of flying and traveling far in a car."

Penelope

SIWA

Top three words that best describe JoJo:

1 Incredible

2 Unstoppable

3 Determined

Fun Fact

These are just a few of the words the girls of XOMG POP! use to describe their mentor, manager, big sister, and second mom, pop superstar JoJo Siwa.

Show 'Em All Who She Is!

FULL NAME: Joelle Joanie Siwa

MY FRIENDS CALL ME: JoJo

BIRTHDAY: May 19, 2003

HOMETOWN: Omaha, Nebraska

ASTROLOGICAL SIGN: Taurus

PETS: A dog named BowBow

SIBLINGS: brother, Jayden Siwa

INSTRUMENTS YOU PLAY: Piano, drums

JOJO'S TOP THREE PIECES OF ADVICE ON BEING A STAR:

1. Try to be really genuine, really be who you are.

2. Chase every dream you have and believe in yourself.

3. Just have fun. Your fans will see that you love what you're doing and love it as well.

JoJo helped create XOMG POP! with her mom, Jessalynn, but her role in the girls' lives doesn't stop there. She invites them to perform with her on tour, choreographs their dances, produces their music, goes on interviews with them, hypes them up before they go onstage, and generally helps them deal with life, career, and fame.

JoJo has surprised the girls with puppies, a day of summer camp, go-cart racing, a trip to Disney, a *whole house* of their very own, AND she even got into a dunk tank for their "Party Like a POP STAR" video release party!

But JoJo's relationship with the girl's isn't all about work and play. It's about the way she genuinely cares about each and every girl in XOMG POP! She's truly like their big sister, best friend, mentor, and mom. As JoJo said on *The Jason Show*, "My girl group is so special, the way they sing and dance . . . it really does feel so special to have . . . these perfect little kiddos that are just owning this world and owning this kid space and setting an example for the next generation."

Now that JoJo and XOMG POP! know they're stronger together, it may just last forever.

TOP THREE WORDS JOJO USES TO DESCRIBE THE GIRLS OF XOMG POP!:

1. HARD WORKING!!!

2. Talented!

3. Sweet, awesome, happy, proud-making, perfect!

JoJo Backstage with the XOMG Girls!

What do Dallas, Brooklynn, Tinie T, and Penelope admire most about JoJo Siwa?

"Her confidence and work ethic! She is a true icon!"

"JoJo works so hard. I think she's pretty much unstoppable, and she always finds ways to better herself. She encourages me to be better, too, and she's really funny."

"I admire her hard work and determination, and I love how she can relate to us or we can relate to her."

"I love that JoJo is hardworking, humble, and a very respectful human being. And no matter what, she always keeps moving forward."

Growing Up Like Bubble Gum!

Pick a pop star! Can you tell which XOMG POP! star is which based on their baby pics?

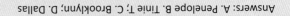

"Telling secrets that we'd never share
Add a little glitter in our hair
Mix in the XOX
Yeah that's how you make a BFF"

What's the best part of being in a girl group managed by JoJo Siwa? Getting to live out your dreams with your very best friends *every single day*!

And the girls of XOMG POP! *know* what makes a BFF phenomenal! Good friends are supportive and honest. They don't judge. And they're *funny*!

Dallas believes being caring and a good listener are important traits in a good friend. Brooklynn knows her honesty, loyalty, and sense of humor make her a friend 1234ever! ((or)) A+ friend material.

Penelope tries to make her friends laugh whenever she can, and she's always there for them when they need her. And Tinie T makes sure her friends keep shining. "When I see my friend is feeling under the weather," she says,

What XOMG POP! lyrics speak to Dallas the most?

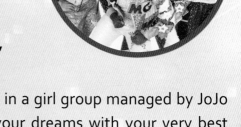

"Any time that I'm in my head
I call my girls 'cause they always said
They tell me, 'Don't be crazy, know
you're amazing'
'Keep on slaying . . .'"

"I always find a way to cheer them up, and I always try to help my friends in any way I can to make sure everyone is doing good."

The girls of XOMG POP! know that no matter what, *real* friends have your back—onstage *and* off. In the early days of the group, the girls were all a little anxious, but they always helped each other out.

As a hip-hop dancer, Tinie T hadn't studied much ballet. So when she got confused in dance class, the other girls helped her mark her turns. And when Penelope joined XOMG POP!, her new best friends helped her catch up *big time.* "They all stepped up and we FaceTimed, and they helped me learn the choreography for a certain song and were so nice about it." The group's encouragement and support even helped Brooklynn ease her fear of elevators!

And the girls *all* supported one another the night before their mega Mall of America performance. *Everyone* was nervous that night! Their rehearsal hadn't gone well so they all gave one another a pep talk and sent encouraging messages in their group chat before the show. And of course, XOMG POP! *crushed* it—*together*!

"And whenever life gets complicated, well, I've got my girls to save me!"

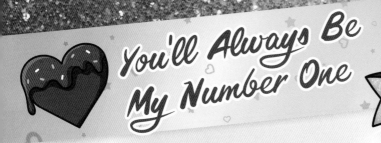

You'll Always Be My Number One

What do we LOVE about our friends in XOMG POP!?

Dallas

1. They are funny and make me laugh.
2. We have each other's backs.

Penelope

1. They have the same sense of humor as me.
2. They are helpful.

Tinie T

1. I love that my friends are always there for me.
2. They always find a way to cheer me up.

Brooklynn

1. Their craziness, and I love how we all act the same and can relate to each other.
2. I love how we have fun.

Fun with Friends

What do we do for fun with our friends?

"I loveeee to go out to eat with them!"
—Brooklynn

"My friends and I like to go to amusement parks together, go-karting, the beach, and other outdoor activities." —Tinie T

"Play Roblox, FaceTime, make Tiktoks, and just be crazy and silly."
—Penelope

"I like to have sleepovers, play games, and film and edit our own movies." —Dallas

TTYLH8RS

Not all friendships are meant to be. Sometimes a *so-called* friend isn't a *true* friend. Brooklynn knows how it feels when a friendship falls apart. "The last time I felt really sad," Brooklynn says, "was when my best friend from Texas didn't wanna be my friend anymore. I had to realize they were not my real friend. My mom made me feel better by taking me out to eat."

What advice would we give a fan who felt left out?

"Keep your head held high and remember your worth. Nobody can take that away from you!"
—Penelope

"If your friends don't like you for who you are, then they aren't real friends, so never change who you are for anybody." —Tinie T

"Be confident in yourself and who you are. Find hobbies and things that make you happy even when you're by yourself."
—Dallas

"Sometimes it's okay to feel alone, and you can be creative in your own way and do what you wanna do."
—Brooklynn

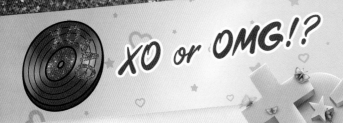

XO or OMG!?

What makes XOMG POP! feel XO?
And what makes us feel OMG!?

	XO	OMG!
Album release party at the Mall of America		Dallas Penelope Tinie T Brooklynn
Getting your XOMG POP! jacket and finding out you made the cut		Dallas Penelope Tinie T Brooklynn

	XO	OMG!
Taking a cruise with your biggest fans	*Dallas* *Penelope*	*Tinie T* *Brooklynn*
Celebrating your birthday with your besties in the band	*Dallas* *Penelope*	*Tinie T* *Brooklynn*
Hanging in the XOMG POP! house		*Dallas* *Penelope* *Tinie T* *Brooklynn*
Hanging with the other members of OMG Pop! after a great show	*Dallas* *Penelope*	*Tinie T* *Brooklynn*

Big Dreams, Big Feelings

"Movin', shakin', can't replicate it
One-of-a-kind, look, Momma, we made it
You've got a dream, believe it and chase it
We're putting our name up in lights."

*B*eing a member of XOMG POP! means living the dream every single day. But being in the spotlight isn't always easy. You miss out on regular kid stuff like going to birthday parties and on field trips, or having sleepovers with friends. People say mean or scary things on social media, they judge you for who you are, and if you mess up, there are hundreds of people watching!

So, what do the girls do to pump themselves up when they're just not feeling it—*YET?!*

Sometimes it's listening to upbeat music—K-pop and Kendrick Lamar work for Brooklynn! Sometimes it's talking through the big feelings with their mom and dad. Most of the time, it involves

How does Penelope pump herself up to perform if she's not feeling peppy? I do my wiggle dance and eat a pixie stick!

"Honestly, it feels great performing. I definitely feel energized by the crowd. It's like the crowd pumps us up even more!" —Brooklynn

taking a step back and giving themselves a pep talk.

Tinie T breaks it down like a beat into three steps: focus, visualization, and feeling the love. First, she focuses on her goals. She asks herself what she wants to accomplish with this performance—whether it's to impress the audience, showcase her skills, or just have fun. Next, she closes her eyes and imagines herself nailing every move and hitting every note perfectly. And finally? She thinks of her fans.

"I remind myself that I have the support of my friends, family, fans, and most importantly, God. Knowing that there are people who believe in me and are rooting for me can be a huge motivator." —Tinie T

"If I'm a little tired before going onstage, I think about the audience and having the best performance. The adrenaline kicks, and I just focus on having fun!" —Dallas

The fans are hands down the biggest energizer for *all* the girls. It's a big change from rehearsing. "Sometimes it is hard getting energy in an empty room," says Brooklynn. But not onstage!

For Penelope, performing on stage in front of a live audience is the *best* feeling ever. "The fans pump you up so much and make you feel so special," she says. "The screaming and smiles make me so hype! It's different than a dance competition because even if you make a mistake, they still love you just the same."

101

Party Like a Pop Star!

What are the MOST AMAZING moments we've had with XOMG POP!—onstage and off?

"An amazing moment was going to **DISNEYLAND** for the first time with the group. It made me feel special because we got to skip all the lines and be escorted around the park. It was memorable because JoJo rode with me and helped me conquer my fear of getting on Space Mountain."

—*Dallas*

"The most amazing moment with XOMG POP! was when we got offstage and celebrated our performance DURING JOJO'S LAST CONCERT OF HER TOUR. It was a huge opportunity for XOMG POP! to perform on the stage with JoJo and be welcomed by such a big and amazing crowd."

—*Tinie T*

"My most amazing moment onstage so far was probably my first time performing with XOMG POP! It made me feel like, 'WOW, I am really a popstar!' I felt so happy! And the most amazing moment offstage was the first time I went to **SIX FLAGS** with XOMG POP! The girls and I got to ride the roller coasters together. It was so much FUN!"

—*Penelope*

"The best offstage moment I would say would have to be **AFTER MALL OF AMERICA**. After we got offstage we all just hugged each other because we did it, we made it, all the hard work we put in finally paid off."

—*Brooklynn*

I Team, I Dream, We're Queens

What makes us feel most creative?

"When I learn something new on recording programs."

Brooklynn

"Music makes me feel most creative."

Tinie T

"What makes me feel most creative is dance."

Penelope

"When I don't have my phone, I get in my creative zone."

Dallas

Reaching for the Stars

If we HAD to be something other than pop stars, what would it be?

"I'd be a producer and write music."
—Brooklynn

"I would like to be an actress, music producer, and artist if I wasn't a pop star." —Tinie T

"I would be a makeup artist and hairstylist." —Penelope

"I'd like to be an actress or a scientist." —Dallas

Think Fast Challenge!

From slime challenges to the Tinie T look-alike fashion show, the girls of XOMG POP! are always coming up with fun challenges for each other—*and* their fans!

Here's a challenge they aced! What's the first thing that popped into the girls' heads when they saw the words below? Bet you can't wait to find out!

CANDY: Sour gummies
NO: Drama
DANCE: Love
PAJAMAS: Silk
PARTY: Fun
PRANK: Tinie T
FRIENDS: Fun
DREAM: XOMG POP!
POP STAR: Cool
BOOGER: Gross

CANDY: Sour Patch Kids
NO: Sleep
DANCE: Hip-hop
PAJAMAS: Silk
PARTY: Invite
PRANK: Wars
FRIENDS: Go
DREAM: Awards
POP STAR: Tinie T
BOOGER: No

Brooklynn

CANDY: Trolli
NO: Sleep
DANCE: Jazz
PAJAMAS: Silk
PARTY: POP STAR
PRANK: Room
FRIENDS: XOMG POP!
DREAM: Grammys
POP STAR: Brooklynn
BOOGER: Nose

Dallas

CANDY: Hearts
NO: Soda
DANCE: Party
PAJAMAS: Comfy
PARTY: Cake
PRANK: Tinie
FRIENDS: Love
DREAM: Big
POP STAR: JoJo
BOOGER: My finger

XOMG POP!

"We are the sparkle queens
Let's show 'em what we all about."

EVERYONE in XOMG POP! rocks their own standout style. From cute and fun to sporty and swaggy and everything in between, the girls of XOMG POP! know how to rock a runway.

Getting all glammed out for a concert *definitely* helps them "get into the pop star mode and feel more confident onstage," as Tinie T likes to say. But the way they dress on a regular day shows the world *EXACTLY* who they are.

Cute

Kawaii style!

Curly hair

Edgy

"I'm fun, easygoing, but still fashionable."

Braids

From my chain collection

Braids for the win!

Plaid 'n' Pink!

Sequins

"Be who you wanna be!"

Boots

"I'm trendy and sporty."

Curly hair

Love my XOMG POP! merch!

"I think it says I am fun and girly!"

Hot pink Pants!

Top Three Favorite Looks!

Ready to get your sparkle on? We're counting down our top three all-time *FAVORITE* looks!

 "Turn your party up, glitter, glitter, yo
We sparkle, sparkle, got that twinkle, twinkle, oh!"

3 Kicking off the countdown at number three is our holiday party look!

 "Because the jacket reminds me of Elton John!" —Dallas

 If you like these looks, check out all the costume changes in our "Moves" video!

2

Coming in at number two are the outfits we wore on JoJo's tour!

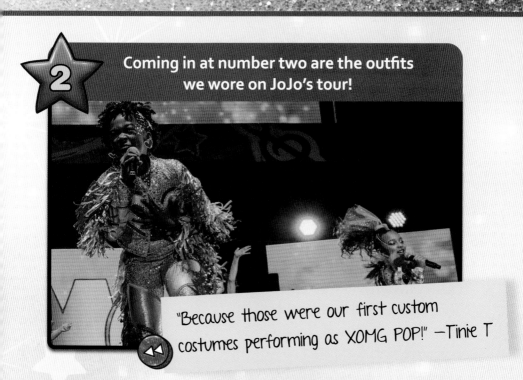

"Because those were our first custom costumes performing as XOMG POP!" —Tinie T

1

And the number one look that wins for fit and style—*boomchikachika, boomchika*, ah— our Mall of America costumes!

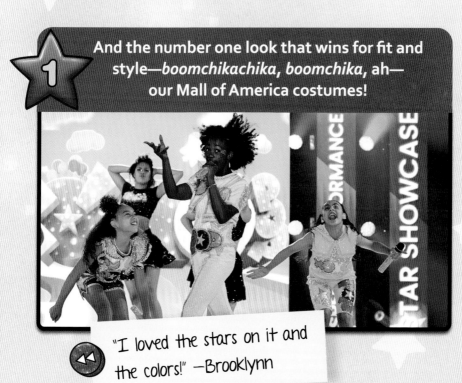

"I loved the stars on it and the colors!" —Brooklynn

Throwing Glitter in the Air

We all know XOMG POP! are the SPARKLE QUEENS, but glitter *ALSO* has a reputation . . . for getting *EVERYWHERE!* What are XOMG POP!'s CRAZIEST glitter disasters, costume calamities, and fashion frictions?

"One time when I was performing, there was a HUGEEE chunk of glitter in my eye and it would not come out. So, I had to do the performance with one eye."

Brooklynn

"One time, I walked past the costume station and they were glittering our costumes, and I knocked down a jar of glitter on the floor. Not one of my proudest moments."

Tinie T

"My worst glitter disaster was when the glitter got into my contacts when performing. That hurt BAD!"

Penelope

"We zip-tie everything, so we usually don't have wardrobe malfunctions. But one time I put a lot of glitter in my hair for a performance, and even after several months and lots of washes, I would still find pieces of glitter in my hair!"

Making the Most of the Mistakes

From tripping and falling with a whole crowd watching to forgetting the lyrics during a video or performance, EVERY girl in XOMG POP!—and the whole entire world, TBH—messes up on the regular. And a big part of being a pop star is knowing how to recover.

So, how do the girls of XOMG POP! handle their bloopers?

Which XOMG POP! lyric makes Tinie T think, *Oh, yes, that's so me?!* "Try to call drop my phone, uhhh, not a crack screen."

What XOMG POP! lyric speaks to Brooklynn the most? "'We'll be laughin', in the future, and living for the bloopers!' because we are all gonna mess up but it's okay. We're just gonna laugh it off."

"I once forgot what to say onstage, so I improvised and it all worked out. And what that taught me is that even if you mess up, just keep on going. Do your best to deliver the best performance and to not let your mistakes bring you down."

"The biggest mistake I made was tripping and almost falling onstage, but I just took a deep breath afterward, trying not to be hard on myself."

"The biggest mistake I ever made onstage was when I forgot the choreography. I just kept smiling and improvising to the music until I caught back on. I learned that it's all about 'the show most go on' and that we are all human and make mistakes."

"The first show on JoJo's tour, I missed my cue because I was so mesmerized by the crowd. I realized what was going on and jumped back in. The only way to get better is to make mistakes and learn from them, and that's how you get better and stronger."

Guess which *MOST* EMBARRASSING MOMENT
EVER belongs to which XOMG Pop Star!

 A I tried to do a card trick for the group, and every time the trick failed. I tried three times and found out later that I was missing two cards!

 B I tripped backstage and fell in front of everyone!

 C I would say when I forgot the lyrics for like four seconds and I had absolutely no clue what was going on.

 D One time when we were rehearsing before a show, we were running the dance and I tripped on my shoelace and fell on my knees.

Answers: A. Dallas; B. Penelope; C. Brooklynn; D. Tinie T

Disco Believers!

Fans Are Life.

**"'Cause we're girls on a mission
To go make a difference."**

It's NO secret that the girls of XOMG POP! have the BEST fans in the whole world. Their fans love and support the group, energize them at concerts, and send them some pretty cool stuff—like a T-shirt for Brooklynn that says "POPSTAR BROOKLYNN," a supercute, handmade bracelet for Penelope, and some really cool things from New Zealand for Dallas. It means so much to the girls that their fans take the time to know them so well!

And the XOMG POP! stars make sure to send all those good vibes right back out into the universe. They've hosted a live dance class at Studio, taken their fans on a cruise, invited them to their album release party at the XOMG POP! house, and launched a phenomenal video campaign with JoJo Siwa and Meghan Trainor to raise money for Dance Against Cancer.

"Life is not always fun and not always happy and all smiles, and so it's really important for me to find the good in every day and spread that to others." —JoJo Siwa

List of Love!

What do we love most about our fans? Here's the short list:

THEY SUPPORT US!

They're so positive!

They're super friendly!

They're LOYAL!

They're honest!

They make great edits!

They're nice!

"There was one fan that came up to us during our meet and greet and said she doesn't have many friends, but she feels like we are her safe space, and she looks up to XOMG POP! so much. That felt like we've reached people's hearts and was a very rewarding experience." —Tinie T

To Our Fans, Thank You!!

"I appreciate my fans so much for all the love and support we receive from [you]. It feels amazing to inspire kids my age to always dream big."

Tinie T

"We wouldn't be where we are without all of you, and we're so grateful. Remember to chase your dreams and follow your heart. You all are amazing and you shine!"

Dallas

"You are appreciated more than you even know. Each and every one of you hold a special place in my heart. You make this all worth it and so much fun! Keep shining and be YOUnique!"

Penelope

"Never forget who you are. XOMG POP! is so grateful for you all, and we would not make it this far without you. I can't wait to share and show you all what's next. You all are very loved."

Love,

Brooklynn

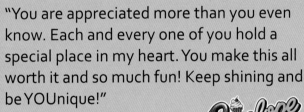

XOMG POP! Quiz! Which XOMG POP! Star Are You Most Like?

YOUR FRIENDS WOULD DESCRIBE YOU AS:

A. Swaggy
B. Sunshine
C. Smart
D. Sweet ((or)) Firecracker

WHAT ARE YOU MOST LIKELY TO WEAR IN YOUR DOWNTIME?

A. Sweatpants and a hoodie
B. Parachute pants and oversized shirts
C. A comfy onesie
D. Sweatpants, T-shirt, and Ugg slippers

YOU HAVE A DAY OFF FROM SCHOOL AND CHORES. HOW DO YOU RELAX?

A. Play electric guitar
B. Lie down on my bed
C. Listen to music or read a book in my clean room
D. Play Roblox in my pajamas

HOW WOULD YOU DESCRIBE YOUR STYLE?

A. Sporty
B. Natural with sunshine and stars
C. Kawaii, cute but edgy
D. Fun and girly

HOW ARE YOU MOSTLY LIKE TO WEAR YOUR HAIR?

A. Down
B. In Bantu knots
C. Up in two buns
D. Curly

WHERE'S YOUR HAPPY PLACE?

A. My very first studio
B. My room
C. My old dance studio
D. Home with family

YOU'RE HAVING A SNACK ATTACK. WHAT DO YOU REACH FOR?

A. Lime-flavored Lays chips
B. Rice cakes
C. Salt and vinegar chips
D. Baked green peas

WHICH CELEBRITY WOULD YOU WANT TO PLAY YOU IN THE MOVIE OF YOUR LIFE?

A. Rihanna
B. Halle Bailey
C. Madison Pettis
D. Taylor Swift

YOUR FAVORITE COLOR IS:

A. Light blue
B. Yellow
C. Purple
D. Hot pink

YOUR BFFS ARE SLEEPING OVER. YOU:

A. Play a prank on them
B. Get them talking. Supporting my friends is the best!
C. Film and edit our own movie
D. Just be crazy and silly

WHAT GIVES YOU THE CHILLS?

A. Loneliness
B. Elevators
C. Spiders
D. Bees. Period!

WHEN YOU TAKE THE STAGE, YOU'RE MOST LIKELY TO

A. Dance hip-hop and rap
B. Win over everyone's heart
C. Sing a soulful solo
D. Be fully of energy and interact with the crowd. I love the fans!

ANSWER KEY

IF YOU ANSWERED MOSTLY A'S,
you're sporty and swaggy, just like your girl Tinie T!

IF YOU ANSWERED MOSTLY B'S,
you're sunshine all day and a star by night, just like Brooklyn!

IF YOU ANSWERED MOSTLY C'S,
you give soulful and smart vibes, just like Dallas!

IF YOU ANSWERED MOSTLY D'S,
your fun, family-first attitude shines bright, just like Penelope!

1234EVER

Look at Her Now

What's up next for the girls of XOMG POP!?

They're gonna keep going beat by beat, step by step. With tours, feature films, outfits, dolls, merch, cartoons, YouTube videos, a cruise with fans, a holiday album, a podcast, and a Dancers for Cancer campaign already under their belts, these sparkle queens are living their dream every single day! And they're sure to be making history as best friends 1234ever!